AMAZING
GRAZING

AMAZING
GRAZING

by Cris Peterson

Photographs by Alvis Upitis

BOYDS MILLS PRESS

Acknowledgements

Thanks to the Ray Marxer, Bob Lee, and Tom Milesnick families for sharing their beautiful ranches and enthusiasm for grazing.

Thanks to Gene Surber, Extension Natural Resources Specialist, Montana State University, for his support and manuscript review.

Thanks to Dayton O. Hyde for the inspiration for this book.

—C.P.

Boyds Mills Press, Inc.
A Highlights Company
815 Church Street
Honesdale, Pennsylvania 18431
Printed in China
Visit our website at: www.boydsmillspress.com

Publisher Cataloging-in-Publication Data

Peterson, Cris.
Amazing grazing / by Cris Peterson ; illustrated by Alvis Upitis.—1st ed.
[32] p. : col. photos. ; cm.
Summary: Three ranches in Montana carry out innovative work in rotational grazing to cultivate healthy ranch lands and streams.
ISBN 1-56397-942-X
1. Rotational grazing — Montana — Juvenile literature. 2. Ranches — Montana — Juvenile literature.
(1. Rotational grazing — Montana. 2. Ranches — Montana. I. Upitis, Alvis. II. Title.
636.0845/ 09786 21   2002   CIP
2001092179

First edition, 2002
Book designed by Amy Drinker, Aster Designs
The text of this book is set in 15–point Janson Text.

10 9 8 7 6 5 4 3 2 1

To the Anderson family,
who loves the American West

—C.P.

To my dear brother, Ilmars, with love

—A.U.

Before the Pilgrims landed at Plymouth Rock in 1620, grasslands covered almost half of North America. Huge herds of bison roamed vast acres of the West eating grass. They often trampled the grass to dust before moving on to fresh pastures.

When ranchers settled the West in the 1800s, their herds of cattle grazed on the very same pastures the bison had roamed. The ranchers never realized the damage their animals could inflict on the land or on the riverbanks. Overgrazing made the land worn out and unproductive. If any good soil remained, it was blown away by the wind or washed away by the rain. Wildlife that depended on the same land for its food became scarce or disappeared altogether.

By the early 1900s, much of the rangeland had been plowed and planted into field crops like corn and wheat. But a terrible drought occurred in the 1930s. The crops burned up in the heat, the destitute farmers left the bare land behind, and much of the topsoil was blown away in awful dust storms.

In recent years, innovative ranchers have changed the way they treat the land and raise beef cattle. To keep their cattle healthy and their grasslands abundant, they know they must take care of the land and the water that flows through it. They have come to realize that the West's largest renewable resource is the green grass that stretches across every mountain valley and rolling hill.

Three Montana ranchers have recently won awards for their dedicated work in caring for the environment by improving the land and the waters of the Western range. Because of their efforts—and the efforts of thousands of other ranchers and farmers across America—the land has healed and become more productive than it has been in centuries. And the wildlife has returned. Seventy-five percent of all wildlife in the United States now lives on privately owned ranches and farms.

How these three Montana ranchers care for their cattle and grasslands to create food, clothing, and a habitat for wildlife is an amazing story.

On many Saturday mornings and during the summer, Trista and Garrett load their horses into a trailer and drive with their mom to the Robert E. Lee Ranch, ten miles from their home in Judith Gap, Montana. Nestled at the foot of the Big Snowy Mountains, the ranch has seven hundred beef cows and their calves. Trista and Garrett love to help out.

At Lee Ranch, Bob Lee and his family have developed a grazing system that involves moving their cattle among

twenty-four pastures. The cattle eat for two or three days in one pasture and then are herded to another one. Since grasslands need to be grazed to remain healthy, the pastures thrive even more than they would have if they had been left untouched.

Bob shows Trista and Garrett how to check the growth of the grass. When it's just the right height, they open a gate and move a herd of eighty pairs of cows and calves into a new area. Trista and Garrett have each been riding horses since they were four years old, and they expertly move the cattle from one pasture to the next.

Different grasses grow at differing rates, so Bob spends considerable time checking the growth of his range. When he moves his animals at just the right time, it helps the grass thicken and keeps the weeds down.

Range grass is an amazing plant that can survive being bitten, cut, stomped on, frozen, and dried out. Its stems are stiff and not very tasty or easy to bite. This helps protect it from overgrazing. When an animal bites off the tip of the grass, the grass continues growing from the bottom. When the grass gets squashed by cattle hooves, it produces a substance that causes the new growth to turn toward the sun.

Cattle are great grazers. Their lips and front teeth gather and cut the grass. Their jagged back teeth grind it into bits.

Tough, chewy stuff that humans could never eat is turned into energy and muscle in the cow's huge body.

Bob and his helpers make sure his herd has adequate water and minerals. In one area of the ranch, Bob drilled a well that supplies a twenty thousand gallon holding tank with fresh water. Then, gravity allows the water to gurgle through an underground pipe four miles long to fill six drinking tanks in the pastures. When Bob creates water sources like this one, his cattle are drawn away from the riverbanks and shallows so they don't trample and damage these fragile areas.

Hundreds of wild birds and animals share the improved grasslands and sparkling streams with the Lee herd. Sharp-tailed grouse, pheasant, and Hungarian partridge nest and raise their young along the creeks on the ranch. Elk and mule deer graze the same pastures as the cattle while mountain lions and coyotes inhabit the uplands near the range.

Matador Ranch

Behind the old red horse barn near the entry to the Matador Cattle Company, Clayton Marxer helps train the horses used to work the cattle on the ranch. His family has lived on the Matador near Dillon, Montana, for twenty-five years. His dad, Ray, manages a herd of seven thousand beef cows and their calves. It's a huge job that requires imagination and lots of experience. The Matador herd grazes on two hundred fifty thousand acres on the eastern slope of the Rocky Mountains, an area nearly one-third the size of Rhode Island.

A small team of colorful cowboys helps Ray and Clayton work the herd. Each spring, they identify all the calves, then vaccinate and brand them. Ray says the brand or mark on each cow's side is her return address. Without a brand to identify which ranch they came from, some of the Matador cattle might end up in Idaho. With an identifiable brand, the wandering cows are almost always returned to their rightful owner.

The Matador range is dry and the grass is sparse, so Ray divides his land into three gigantic pastures. His "black

baldie" cattle, black stocky animals with white faces, graze on one pasture each year. A second pasture rests, and the third is grazed only after the grass seeds have ripened on the plants. As the cattle meander through that pasture, they knock off the plant seeds with their legs. Then they trample the seeds into the soil as they chomp on the grass. The indentations their hooves make in the dirt help catch the rainfall, so the newly "planted" seeds can sprout.

As the mountain snows begin to melt each spring, nearly every cow on the Matador gives birth to a new calf. Within its first hour of life, each fuzzy new arrival totters to its feet and nudges its mother until it finds her milk. Within a day or two, cow and calf are let out onto the range. While the mother cow grazes, her calf nurses on her fresh milk up to seven times a day. After two or three weeks, the newborns begin to nibble on tender shoots of grass, too.

Along with the thousands of grazing cattle, an assortment of wildlife lives on the Matador. A set of triplet pronghorn antelope graze the range with the cattle. Moose, wolves, and bear inhabit the uplands while deer browse on the pastures near the ranch buildings. Sandhill cranes, hawks, and golden eagles soar overhead.

Molly and Meghan are learning to fish with their dad along the East Gallatin River that runs through the heart of Milesnick Ranch, near their home. Each summer, more than fifteen hundred fly fishermen travel from all over the country to fish the creeks and rivers that crisscross this ranch on the edge of Belgrade, near Bozeman, Montana.

Tom Milesnick and his family spend considerable time and effort restoring the streams on their ranch to provide the best habitat for trout. Trout only thrive in clean, crystal-clear water. If you look closely, you can see them lazily swimming near a bend in one stream.

Tom's five hundred cows and their calves graze on the lush grasses in eighteen pastures, or cells, as he calls them. After eating for two or three days, the cattle are moved to a new area.

While Molly and Meghan fish, the herd moves in to graze on the riverbanks nearby. Short-term grazing helps improve the trout streams by keeping the grass healthy, so it holds the soil and maintains the banks. Tom moves the cattle out of this area after only eight hours.

Each summer, Tom drives his truck out to the pasture, climbs up a tall ladder on the truck bed, and photographs key areas of his ranch. By comparing pictures taken over several years, he can detect whether the creek banks are changing or weeds are invading. He can also identify small changes that may be developing on the pastures. He uses this information to decide when to graze a cell and for how long.

A small flock of pelicans stretch their enormous wings and noisily fly up from one of the streams. Pelicans only visit in the spring, but mallards and

other species of ducks nest near the creeks and spend a good part of the summer there. Eagles and ospreys swoop over the pastures hunting for small rodents.

The Milesnicks' attention to detail on their ranch has helped them create an environment that is healthy for cattle. It also preserves a unique natural resource that their many visitors can enjoy.

These three Montana families share the same goals as thousands of ranchers and farmers across America—to preserve an environment of abundant grasslands and clean, flowing streams where their cattle can thrive. They work hard to protect and improve these natural resources. Bob, Ray, and Tom have garnered national recognition for their conservation efforts. But to them the

real reward is having healthy cows, a sound environment,
and thriving wildlife in a place where the wide open
heritage of the American West survives.